# THIS GRACE WHEREIN WE STAND

## THE WARRACK LECTURES

# THIS GRACE
# WHEREIN WE STAND

By
GEORGE JOHNSTONE JEFFREY
D.D.

HODDER & STOUGHTON
Limited   London

*To*
ARCHIE and AILEEN,
IAN and MARGARET

*First Printed 1949*

MADE AND PRINTED IN GREAT BRITAIN
FOR HODDER AND STOUGHTON LIMITED
BY JARROLD AND SONS LTD., NORWICH

# PREFACE

THESE Lectures were delivered to the students of New College, Edinburgh, and St. Mary's College, St. Andrews, in the spring of 1948. To Principal Watt and Principal Duncan and their staffs of professors, my warm thanks are due for their courtesy and co-operation. I have preserved the direct form in which the addresses were delivered.

The only way in which one could have the courage to accept the Committee's invitation to deliver a series of lectures on preaching, where the ground had been covered so adequately by outstanding predecessors was to forget all about them and be oneself. It is in this spirit that these pages are offered to any who may find them suggestive.

To Rev. Wm. S. Buchan, B.D., and the Publications Committee of the Church of Scotland I am indebted for their permission to use here the chapter on "The Minister's Devotional Life", which I contributed to *The Minister's Manual*.

My special thanks are due to Mrs. Jessie A. Reid, for the meticulous care she brought to the typing and editing of the Lectures in preparation for publication.

GEO. JOHNSTONE JEFFREY

GLASGOW.
*November 1948.*

5

# CONTENTS

# Chapter I

## OUR PERENNIAL THEME

IN the preaching of the word, there are granted to the commonest of us certain never-to-be-forgotten days when, for once, we become inspired men and know the supreme exhilaration of mediating to our fellows the redeeming passion of the Son of God. One can conceive but one other human experience analogous to it—a rapture some of you have known—a young airman's first solo flight. Such red-letter days in the pulpit are for ever memorable, setting a standard for all future efforts. Of course, the thing is a miracle. On that day we know, with a kind of awe, that it has pleased God to transpierce our common clay with supernatural power, setting His treasure in earthen vessels. Within the limits of our personality, we are used of God to the uttermost. The apt word leaps to clothe the healing thought. The atmosphere is tense with the moving of the Spirit. Every worshipper is conscious that here is no mere human word but an authentic word of God to his deepest need. We have become spiritually airborne, lifted to a height where human praise were a sacrilege, and even thanks an unlawful intrusion. We learn what that meaneth— "He maketh his angels spirits, his ministers a flaming fire", and, in breathless wonder and humility, we ask ourselves if anything like this can ever happen again.

Lest you imagine that this is mere rhapsody, allow me, striving towards the same goal, to present the obverse side of the picture. There are days in preaching when we strike rock-bottom and, for a man of any spiritual sensitiveness, life holds few such humiliations. A preacher's failure is such a public failure. Moreover, it is easy to mistake wounded vanity for sincere contrition. Add to this that our very ascent into the pulpit raises hopes in expectant souls. Spiritually-minded folks are there, eager to know more of the love of God in all its length and breadth and depth and height. The doubting and the perplexed are there, who will be grateful beyond words for any light your message may shed on their confusions. Some youth may be there, with a hidden vulture of temptation burying its beak in his vitals. Above all, the sorrowing are there, strained to breaking point by loss or bereavement. Woe be to us if we dash these fervid hopes to the ground and, for bread, offer a stone. George Eliot speaks of the sin of tearing down the altar of trust we have built up in human hearts. Let our grave responsibility be burned into us by our culpable failure in the pulpit, knowing that it is this serious condemnation of which we are guilty when we face an expectant congregation shamefully unprepared. Doubtless these failures can happen even when we have toiled and prayed and striven—but these are the exceptions.

Usually the reasons are not far to seek. There is a wistful saying of Dr. Johnson's as he reviewed a certain portion of his past. "This is not the kind of life to which heaven is promised." And by the same token there are passages in our own secret life unto God, when we are constrained to confess "This is not the kind of life to which great preaching is promised." It has been well said that "the test of a vocation is the love of the drudgery it involves". Few of us can hear the saying without a stab of conscience. Two or three more hours of hard, honest work on a sermon would have redeemed it from mediocrity and made it a finished weapon in the hand of God. There are other reasons, all too obvious to God though hidden from man, why the divine fires within us smoulder and sink in their own ashes. By inner treacheries and compromises, we cut ourselves off from the sources of divine power. The only preaching that is owned and blessed of God is that which grows out of the daily discipline of our lives. Triumphant preaching is the fruit of victorious living. Every day we stand as at the dividing of two roads, the one the hard, narrow path ascending to the shining, white peaks of the spirit; the other, the broad, sweet, downward vistas of the flesh. It should be said, plainly and austerely, at the outset, that the issue of this warfare concerns not ourselves alone. It will leave its mark on every sermon we preach. Lack of self-discipline, failure to capture the fleeting, fertile mood, perfunctory devotions, treacherous procrastinations—

9

this is not the hinterland whence flows the preaching that changes lives. Here, as everywhere, "what a man soweth, that shall he also reap." Purity of motive, prevailing prayer, sweat of brain and heart, these will be given back to us in our preaching with mathematical exactitude. Without them, the oncoming of the Lord's Day can never be anything but a certain fearful forward-looking unto judgment. Inspired by them, preaching may be life's joy and crown.

And now let us return to the positive note on which we set out. There are, it seems to me, four aspects of our vocation which should fan the holy flame. The first is:

*The exceeding greatness of the Gospel committed to our charge.* The sense of its greatness will, of course, rise and fall with our veering moods, but a sustained belief in its glorious adequacy to man's utmost need is a first essential for every ambassador of Christ.

We are all familiar with Shakespeare's great lyrical outburst of patriotism, working up to its exulting climax:

> This royal throne of kings, this sceptred isle,
> This earth of majesty, this seat of Mars,
> This other-Eden, demi-Paradise,
> This precious stone, set in the silver sea,
> This blessed plot, this earth, this realm, *this England.*

There is another patriotism and a greater, a holy, flaming fire in the heart of every true preacher. With

what abandon would its greatest exponent exclaim
"*This grace wherein we stand*," and what jubilant content would he give it. "This inner world of privilege
and blessedness and conviction, its citizens the redeemed of all ages, its anointed King holding in thrall
the best spirits of each succeeding generation, this
Kingdom with its own laws, at once benignant and
inexorable, this realm where nothing is bought or sold
or earned, but where all is without money and without
price, this land of freedom purchased at such a ransom,
this high calling whereof we are made ministers, this
grace wherein we stand." Without this dominating
passion of allegiance, no man is fit to preach the Christ
of God. Without this joyous compulsion we go forth,
maimed men, to an "engagement very difficult."
Aflame with it, we ride out conquering and to
conquer.

The second aspect of our calling which should strike
fire from us is:

*The desperate challenge of this devastated world.* Its
ruin and rubble are but the outward symbols of
its inward bankruptcy. As it has been said, "An
awful solemnity is upon the earth, for the last
vestige of earthly security is gone. It has always been
gone and religion has always said so, but we haven't
believed it." True, but men are believing it to-day.
Mankind perishes with hunger. Let its dark tragedy
beget in us a passion to serve its distresses and necessities. The remedy we propose for this mortal sickness

is, has always been, and will always be, to the outsider, a theme for scorn. Confronted with the cataclysm of these tragic years, it is laid on us once more to prove that the foolishness of God is wiser than the wisdom of men. There was a period in the late war when Germany was at the zenith of her evil power. Her spokesman, the infamous Goebbels, in a characteristic broadcast, smirking sardonically behind the piled-up German armaments and waving aside contemptuously every consideration of the Spirit, exclaimed: "You cannot build an empire on moonbeams." On such a conviction he and his like proceeded to found an empire that was to last a thousand years. Time has graven its awesome epitaph on such an ideology. *"You cannot build an empire on moonbeams!"* That is precisely what we Christians propose to do—to build a new world, having in its structure the implications of eternity, and to build it on things not seen with the eye nor grasped with the hand, on things filmy, intangible, imponderable, on everlasting principles of righteousness, justice, reverence for human personality —above all, on healing, redemptive love. We have seen, on a world scale, the vanity of the material and the triumph of the eternal. A burning conviction that we have in our message the divine response to man's need must banish from our preaching all that is bleak and sombre and feebly apologetic. The issue for the world which must be the passion of all our preaching has been set forth in the words of T. S. Eliot:

> The only hope or else despair
> Lies in the choice of pyre or pyre,
> To be redeemed from fire by fire
> We only live, only suspire
> Consumed by either fire or fire.

The challenge of to-day can only be answered when the pentecostal flames once more descend upon our heads. The absence of this glow in our preaching cannot be hid. Burne Jones attended the funeral service of Robert Browning and, as a memorial of that doughty spirit, found it woefully unworthy, drab and cheerless to a degree. Said he, "I would have given something for a banner or two, and I would have given much if a chorister had come out and rent the air with a trumpet." Unless we have this clarion note in our preaching to-day, unless we believe that, against the massed forces of evil, we have with us the triumphant fulness of God, we cannot claim to be the heralds of One who had the right to say "I have overcome the world." Get it wrought into the fibres of your being that surging up from the depths of the heart of God are resources for man's redemption which are both irresistible and inexhaustible. In the city of Bath there are springs of healing water, rising from a depth of five thousand feet. Since long before Roman times these waters, we are told, have flowed on to this day, their virtue unimpaired, their volume unabated, their heat undiminished. It is in terms like these that the preacher is to think of the Gospel of Jesus Christ, the

Son of God. It was thus that the greatest apostle conceived it—as a glorious crescendo. "God is able," we can hear him declaring, "able to do", "able to do all", "able to do above all", "able to do abundantly above all", "able to do exceeding abundantly above all that we ask or think, according to the power that worketh in us." So said Paul and, in his own character and world conquests, he had every right to say it. And we also shall have the same assurance when we too offer Christ our undivided allegiance and our unreserved obedience, and the fire in us will kindle the sacred fires in others.

Thirdly, once more there has been displayed before us on a world-wide canvas, the picture of *man's utter failure to work out his own salvation*. For us as preachers, this is to be, literally, the chance of a lifetime. Few people to-day, contemplating world ruin without and the moral chaos of their own hearts, are blaring forth the claim to be masters of their fate and captains of their soul. Wherever a man will be honest with himself, he knows that this pseudo-confidence and this dubious complacency are a mere façade, a pasteboard screen to hide from others and from himself, his own inner defeats, inadequacies and self-deceptions. For a typical example of this foundation of sand, I refer you to a significant passage in that powerful and disturbing novel *South Riding*, by Winifred Holtby. Of that efficient young woman, Sarah Burton, who has shed from her shoulders what she considers the incubus

14

of her parents' evangelical faith, the writer says: "To be washed in the blood of the Lamb appeared to her a nauseating exercise. Confession and absolution she thought to be an evasion of personal responsibility. Redemption she considered a task for the individual will. Life was what each man made it." It is long since one has come upon such a scornful manifesto of the unregenerate human heart. One can but ask whether, after passing through the fiery furnace of sordid temptation described with such stark realism in a later chapter of the novel, she would subscribe with equal jauntiness to her self-sufficient creed. Beaten to her knees, I am bound to think, she would be in no mood to make sardonic comments on evangelical phraseology concerning the blood of the Lamb. It might begin to dawn upon her that there are worse methods of stating the fact that desperate diseases require desperate remedies and, in her moral and spiritual bankruptcy, would be only too willing, like countless others, to confront herself with the offence of the Cross. As for confession and absolution, the longer you are in the ministry and the more you know of the human heart, the more surely will you discover that their name is legion who, beneath all appearances to the contrary, are trembling on the verge of confession and are aching for any physician who can "cleanse the stuffed bosom of that perilous stuff, that weighs upon the heart." So far from redemption being a task for the individual, our present world plight and our humiliating, perennial and foredoomed failure to save ourselves by any strength of our own have proved it of all tasks the most hopeless. So far from life being "what each man makes it," so far from claiming to be self-made men, we Christians can but say like the Apostle, out of an abysmal gratitude for the everlasting mercy, "It is by the grace of God that I am what I am."

*"This grace wherein we stand."* There is your theme and your inspiration for a lifetime, the preaching, with glowing and growing conviction, of God's free, unmerited mercy in Christ Jesus to the sinful sons of men. The absence of this joyous confidence cannot be hid. It is the reason for the failure of much of our modern preaching. Joy alone can beget joy. Denney quotes Dale as noting the one defect in the preaching of that great, spiritually-minded man, Pusey. "In parting with the Lutheran truth concerning justification, he parted with the springs of gladness." Fairbairn emphasises this defect when he says: "For Pusey, sin was more a matter for himself to bear than for Christ to remove." The preaching of to-day, it seems to me, must rediscover these springs of gladness. These alone will make our message vibrant, convincing, contagious. They reach down to the eternal, deeper far than the shifting emphases and changing vogues of theological speculation. It is good to return to the famous preachers who have spent their lives in delivering themselves of this great gospel enfranchisement. If you wish

16

to find a glowing example of it, read and re-read that chapter in Principal Hugh Watt's *Life of Thomas Chalmers*, entitled "The Awakening of Kilmeny." The man whose nature does not leap into a flame at these pages was never intended to preach the gospel. I am not ashamed to confess that the reading of this chapter is part of my own preparation for sitting down at the table of Christ's dying, undying love. We must, as never before, be flamingly sure that we have a gospel to preach which has this hallmark of glad contagiousness in every throb of it. One hears so many sermons where Christ is held up to us as nothing more than the Great Exemplar. In its place, that is important—even vital—but it is not the first place. If Christ came merely for our example, if the Christian life consists in nothing more than trying to batter and bruise ourselves into being like Him, then He came not for our salvation but for our despair. The desire for Christ-likeness is most praiseworthy, but it is "the desire of the moth for the star." Christlikeness, if it comes, reaches us by another avenue. Set out on the Christian ministry telling yourselves a few simple, elementary things. Get to know the world of difference between "Pay me what thou owest" and "I frankly forgave thee all," between "Make you a new heart and a new spirit," and "A new spirit will I give you," or as Dr. James Moffatt once put it, in words as simple as they are profound: "We are not saved because we are good: we are good because we are saved." Thus only shall we learn that Christlikeness is not something we achieve. It is something God sets aglow in humble, forgiven hearts.

Lastly, your task is to preach *the unchanging Christ in a changing world*. Written all over man's history are the words, "Everything changes, nothing changes." We live in an amazing world of inventions and discoveries beyond the wildest dreams of our forefathers to conceive, and the changes that are bound to come as science conquers reach after reach of the unknown, baffle our imagination. "Everything changes" but, in a far deeper sense, "nothing changes." There abide these human hearts, with their perennial hunger and thirst. If they truly knew themselves, they would say "Show us Christ and it sufficeth us." Here, then, is another aspect of your high calling—preaching, in a superficially changing world, Him who is the same yesterday, to-day and forever. There are those who gravely doubt if the thing can be done. In his Gifford Lectures, *The Human Situation*, Professor MacNeile Dixon says: "Can anyone tell us whether Christ would have approved of the pattern of our present civilisation and, if not, how are we to escape from it? Would He have approved of costly and magnificent churches, gorgeous ritual and music, of the theatre and the picture-house? Can anyone tell us unequivocally what would have been His attitude to athletics, to birth-control, to sterilisation of criminals and the unfit, or to capital punishment?" It is interesting to compare these words with others of Dean Inge: "It is not likely that Jesus would say the same things in the twentieth century that He said in the first. It is certain that He attached little value to the accessories of civilisation. He disliked luxury which diverts the mind from higher things, multiplying cares and complicating life to no purpose. He would have been quite uninterested in automobiles and aeroplanes. But everything that makes human nature better would have had His warm approval." Now, without trying to settle the differences implied in these two opinions, is it not enough to say that Jesus left behind Him no exhaustive catalogue of possible human situations and problems with His categorical "yea" or "nay" affixed to each? That way lay the legalism and casuistry He came to annul. What He did leave were certain eternal principles illuminating the spirit and the understanding, entrusting the application of them to the consensus of Christian conscience and intelligence. But what I would stress in closing is this. Beneath everything that confronted mankind was its primary need of help more than human, something fundamental and revolutionary, without which nothing stable and eternal could be built. It is with these elementary and supernatural things that you are to be concerned for a lifetime. Christ is the Great Contemporary. He is ever bringing forth fresh light from His Gospel—the Gospel it will be your privilege to expound and commend to human hearts. Go out in good hope and strong confidence to preach things old and new. So may you serve your day and generation in the will of God.

> Him evermore I behold
> Walking in Galilee,
> Through the cornfields waving gold,
> In hamlet and grassy wold,
> By the shores of the beautiful sea.
> He toucheth the sightless eyes.
> Before Him the demons flee.
> To the dead He sayeth "Arise"
> To the living "Follow Me".
> *And that voice still soundeth on*
> *From the centuries that are gone*
> *To the centuries that shall be.*

# CHAPTER II

## PREACHING RESOURCES

TO-DAY we consider the three main sources of Christian preaching. The first, obviously, is

### The Bible.

Let it be said at the outset that we shall deal with the Scriptures almost exclusively as a great human document, with such a unique knowledge of our hearts that we can only trace its inspiration to God who made them. If I do not dwell here on its doctrinal aspects, it is because it is the business and privilege of your professors and lecturers to do so, even amid a curriculum all too brief and overcrowded. No words of mine can sufficiently describe the vital importance for preaching of such discipline and training. Unless you set out into the ministry of to-day under the great, overarching conception of the Incarnation of God in Christ Jesus, and all that is implied in that divine revelation, you will spend your days, spiritually and homiletically, in the shallows. Yours will be a hand-to-mouth existence which makes the ministry a vexatious and disabling penury. Rooted and grounded in the great experimental truths of the Christian faith, you may often be straitened in yourselves but never in

God. There could be nothing more ironic than the spectacle of a young minister going forth to preach in a world like this, with an experience of the Gospel that is nothing more than a flabby pietism. Such an one is woefully ignorant of the problems of a broken world in the throes of re-birth, even more of the solution of them. A word which was frequently on the lips of our revered teacher, Dr. Denney, was the word "relevant". With what impatience would he say of some line of thought, "All this is hopelessly irrelevant to the main issue." There are so many goodish folks in the world who need this caution! For years I had the skilled attention of a lady chiropodist. The day came when she had to retire on account of age, and she wished to recommend another lady. But the testimonial she gave me failed to impress: "She is a fine Christian worker!" I did not wish to hurt the dear old lady's feelings, but, of course, any day I prefer the help of an agnostic who knows something of chiropody to that of the finest "Christian worker" who bleeds my toes! Seriously, the young minister who affects to despise theology is in for a rude awakening. This devastated world bristles with problems which do not admit of mere pietistic simplification. They call for profound and disciplined theological scholarship, sweat of brain as well as warmth of heart.

But, as I have said, it is for its incomparable knowledge of the heart of man that we return continually to this sacred book. Above all others, it pierces beneath every distinction and difference in life—rank, wealth, education and prestige, and sets the deepest recesses of the heart in the white light of the scrutiny of God. On its every page it anticipates the Judgment Day, when many that are first shall be last, and the last first. Ever old, it is ever new—uniquely applicable to each human emergency. This is true in every great crisis, international, national and individual. Some of us have lived through two armistice days which brought to an end two appalling wars. No great poet had to arise to express our sense of awesome deliverance. Wherever men gathered in crowded churches to express their undying gratitude to the Divine Deliverer, they found words to hand, written ages ago but new and spontaneous for this special crisis. "If it had not been the Lord who was on our side when men rose up against us, the stream had gone over our soul, then the proud waters had gone over our soul. Our soul is escaped as a bird out of the snare of the fowlers. The snare is broken and we are escaped." To take another example, re-living the long agony of the war years and trying to interpret at least some of God's ways with man, do we not see, flashing out from page after page of this book, some piercing insight into, some working solution of, a desperate mystery? Confronted with God's seeming inaction against inhuman barbarity, we learned what that meaneth: "The face of the Lord is against them that do evil," the face, not meantime the hands: God waiting and watching, while evil men filled up

23

the cup of wickedness, till the day came when He bared His arm and brought down the stupendous edifice of villainy. Even more awesome, to many minds, was that day of retribution when a score of men who had strutted as gods upon the earth, wielding the power of life and death over millions of their fellows, sat in the dock at Nuremberg, confronted at long last with their guilt and infamy. Can we not see the searchlight of God on their blanched faces, can we not hear the voice of God, in tones of thunder, pronouncing sentence on their fiendish deeds? "These things thou hast done, and I kept silence. Thou thoughtest that I was altogether such an one as thyself, but I will convict thee and set them in order before thine eyes." These are but a few examples from Scripture of the timeliness and timelessness, the appositeness and the finality of God's dealings with the nations of men.

Again, the same impressiveness reveals itself in the Bible in showing God's part *in individual lives*. Here is a book, above all others, which teaches that for none of us is there such a thing as privacy, that what to us is dark, to Him is open day, that in our highest moments, when we ascend unto Heaven, He is there, and in our lowest fall, when we make our bed in Hell, He is there. When this sense of God, as the Great Searcher of hearts, deepens in us with the years, then, with the Bible in our hands, we need never be at a loss for that spiritual insight which is the first requisite of the true preacher. Let me dwell on one or two examples of this kind of insight. Here is the brave, proud Naaman, who feels it is due to one in his exalted position that he should be saved in state. Watch the prophet dealing one sledge-hammer blow after another at his pride, till he learns at last "the blessedness of being little", so that "he went down and dipped himself seven times in Jordan, according to the saying of the man of God, and his flesh came again like unto the flesh of a little child, and he was clean." Contemplate also David the King, in the aftermath of his great sin. Watch him seeking to lay the flattering unction to his soul that he would be bold indeed who would dare to question the private life of a king. See the quiet man steal into his presence with his childlike tale of the rich man and the ewe lamb. Hear David pouring out his indignation against one capable of such a dastardly deed. Then, like a lightning flash, see the disclosure of David's black crime, as the prophet holds up the mirror to his deepest soul. "Look at yourself. Thou art the man." Take as a final example an incident from the New Testament. Not in any kindness of heart, but in a spirit of sneering condescension, a Pharisee asks Jesus to dine with him. "There now," is his inmost thought, "there is a good dinner for you, a thing you don't get every day. Now let me hear you talk." And Jesus did talk, in a way His hearer remembered till his dying day. "Simon, I have somewhat to say unto thee." "To me?" he says, in a kind of shocked surprise. "To this soiled woman, perhaps, but to me, a master

25

in Israel?" And Jesus goes on to say to him something piercing, intimate, personal, and before He has done with him he is made to learn that this untouchable knows more of the great, Fatherly heart of God than was contained in all the counsels of the Sanhedrin.

Such, gentlemen, is the book which is to be the unfailing fountain of all your preaching. This insight into human motive and character is the open proof of its divine inspiration. "Truly the word of God is quick and powerful, and sharper than a two-edged sword, piercing even to the dividing asunder of soul and marrow, and is a discerner of the thoughts and intents of the heart."

Our second source of inspiration for preaching is found in *the hearts of those committed to our pastoral charge*. One of the outstanding consequences of the Damascus experience for the Apostle is implied in his words: "Henceforth I know no man after the flesh." Before his conversion, learning, social standing, rank and prestige, personal appearance—all these had bulked large in Paul's estimate of his fellows. But when the great revolution came in his thinking and in his life, he had the habit of stripping human beings of all extraneous trappings and uncovering their desperate need of God. Henceforth, he saw a man no longer as rich or poor, learned or unlearned, but as one in whose inmost soul was proceeding a drama of the conflict between good and evil, with issues stretching out to all eternity. We must sit at the feet of Jesus Christ and the great Apostle that we may learn this deep insight into the hearts of our people. We ministers, with the growing years, know the truth of Mark Rutherford's words: "I have been taught, over and over again, that unknown abysses into which the sun never shines, lie covered with commonplace in men and women, and are revealed only by the rarest opportunity." The true preacher is one who takes endless pains in studying, with ever-deepening interest, the hopes and fears, the motives—so strangely mingled, the evasions, the inarticulate longings, the thirst for the living God found in the hearts of those entrusted to our pastoral care. As an approach to this kind of discipline, words of Spinoza are full of wisdom. "I have taken sedulous care not to ridicule human actions, not to bemoan them, not to hate them, but to understand them." Such training is specially necessary for men in the ministry whose temperament is of the over-introspective type. For them there is always a subtle temptation to regard their people as little more than the necessary audience for their sermons. They constantly tend to put books before men. It is possible to emerge from our studies where, like Peter, we have been sitting by the fire and warming ourselves, with eyes half-closed to the engrossing drama of human personality lying near to our own doors. If we move among our people with eyes and ears and heart fully open, we shall never fail of the material for that warm, intimate, comforting preaching for which the hungry soul is for ever crying out. There is no minister here who could not give stirring examples of this fruitful human contact, with their harvest for helpful preaching. It is part of the real romance of our calling that even a casual encounter with an ordinary man or woman may provide for us one of the most memorable sermons we may ever deliver. With some diffidence, I wish to give a few examples from my own human contacts. As I have said, every minister can furnish instances of these experiences by which sermons grow. Sometimes they can be almost uncanny in their timeliness. I was working on a sermon on the text, "The witnesses laid down their clothes at a young man's feet, whose name was Saul." I was tracing the effect of the death of Stephen on the mind of Saul of Tarsus, the unconscious undermining of his ancient faith by the sight of this cruel deed, and his, largely unwilling, admiration for the new faith that could inspire such a heroic death. I sought to show that all this was but the gradual loosening of the avalanche which gave way at last on the Damascus road. In the midst of this preparation for the coming Sunday, a cultured young lady teacher had occasion to call on me. I noticed, in the course of conversation, that she kept—to my mind strangely and unnecessarily—bringing in the name of a man on the same staff, and that in a rather critical and bitter way. All at once the truth flashed upon me. *She was in love with the man and did not know it.* She was trying to fight down an emotion she did not understand. Sure enough, she shortly afterwards became engaged to him and they were very happily married. Here was a human illustration of the experience of many a youth in his relation to Jesus Christ. The main problem in the ferment of youth may not always be intellectual doubt but rather resistance to the pressure of a great beseeching love.

Then how many sayings we have listened to in an ordinary day's going find their niche in our sermon preparation. A friend passed on to me a snatch of conversation with another man who, all unconsciously, gave away the real character of his relations with God. With an unctuous shake of the head, the latter exclaimed: "Yes, God has been very good to me, but then, *I've been very good to Him!*" (Denney used to say, "The worst of speaking without thinking is that you say what you think.") Here was a man who was unaware that his relationship with God could only be described as "Religion on a Cash Basis." It made a foil for the real attitude to God as emblemed in God's word to Abraham: "I am thy exceeding great reward" —not flocks, and herds, and material success, but more of Myself, the truth that a spiritual man shall receive a spiritual man's reward.

In the early days of the First World War, I met a youth in my congregation, straight from the trenches and burdened with his full fighting kit. On my asking him how far he felt he could march under such a load, he replied like a canny Scot, "Maybe twelve miles," and then added, "fifteen *with a band*," a flashlight, surely, on a great text—"Thy statutes have been my songs in the days of my pilgrimage."

A last instance. In one of my charges my visitation took me frequently to the bedside of a suffering man. There were days when he was utterly depressed by his painful malady. But there were others when one saw in his whole bearing the triumph of the spirit over the flesh. He wist not that his face shone. He was a shy, diffident man, not in the least glib or voluble regarding the mysteries of religion, but one day, seeing the look of wonder in my eye at his manifest transfiguration, he said quietly, in his strong, native Scots: "You see, it's like this. Him and me hae been very chief this week." (Christ and I have been very intimate this week.) Here was a man vastly ignorant of human learning, but deep in the arcana of God, a true mystic though he would not have known what the word meant.

Let us go about among our fellows with the seeing eye, the hearing ear, and the understanding heart, and scarcely a week will pass that will not provide for us some apt illustration of some great Biblical truth.

Lastly, there are *the preaching resources which lie deep in our own hearts*. And here I would make a strong plea. Learn to believe in your own experience and let your hearers have the benefit of it. One reason why those who listened to Jesus said of Him, "We never heard it after this fashion," was that He did not, with any false modesty, keep quoting Rabbi this and Rabbi

30

that. He spoke with utter confidence out of His own first-hand experience of God. The spiritual was His native air. Here also, with humility and yet with confidence, let us follow His example. Consecrate to your preaching your own loneliness. There are words of Robertson of Brighton, in one of his greatest sermons, which every preacher should take to heart—I had almost said "should know by heart". "Let life be a life of faith. Do not go timorously about, enquiring what others think, what others believe, what others say. It seems the easiest, it is the most difficult thing in life to do this. Believe in God. God is near you. Throw yourself fearlessly upon Him. Trembling mortal, there is an unknown might within your soul which will wake when you command it. The day may come when all that is human, man or woman, will fall off from you as they did from Him. Let His strength be yours. Be independent of them all now. The Father is with you. Look to Him and He will save you."

I have said: consecrate to your preaching your own loneliness, every original gift of personality you possess. Never be afraid to declare to others what God has done for your soul. It can be done wisely and humbly, without the least suspicion of egotism. And I would go on to add this: let God make use of your deficiencies and handicaps. We may have to deplore the absence of certain desirable gifts of personality. We may have some humiliating defect of temperament. Our natures may be very difficult to manage. There is nothing more wonderful in the economy of God than the way in which He can use for His high purposes a nature outwardly unattractive. I quote at length what I consider the supreme example of this. A writer has left behind him an impression of Abraham Lincoln's first appearance at an important gathering in New York. He described the great liberator's lean face and awkward mien, his big hands, his ill-fitting, badly wrinkled clothes, his large ears, his uncouth gestures and provincial accent. "When I first saw him, and still more, when I heard his opening sentences, I said to myself, 'Old fellow, this won't do. This may be all very well for the Wild West. It will never go down in New York.' But very soon he seemed to catch fire. He straightened up, made regular and graceful gestures. His face was lit up. The whole man was transfigured. I forgot his clothes, his peculiarities, his personal appearance. Then I forgot myself, and I was on my feet like the others, cheering to the echo, when he reached his climax, amid thunders of applause. I came out quivering with excitement. A friend asked me, 'What do you think of Abraham Lincoln, the backwoodsman?' I said, 'He is the greatest man since St. Paul,' and I think so yet."

Lastly, let God use in your preaching your own wrestlings, and defeats, and sorrows. George Eliot found the secret of the strange healing power of Thomas a' Kempis' *Imitation of Christ* in the fact that "it was not written by one reclining on velvet cushions for those walking the hard, stony way with bleeding feet." A minister has to be prepared for his own crosses, periods of financial strain, of ill health, of doubts and depressions, of family anxieties, it may be sore bereavement, and, to the end of the road, that struggle between the flesh and the spirit to which we are all conscript. For your heartening here, we older men can predict that it is out of this grim travail that some of your greatest sermons will be born. If a man is carrying through a ministry of wonderful comfort, depend upon it he is knowing, in his own heart, sorrow and the means of transfiguring it. One has often watched, with bated breath, a huge yacht on our River Clyde, with its mighty spread of white sail. In a sudden squall it heels over until it seems but the work of a second to capsize it. But one learns to smile at fears like these. Anyone who has seen such a vessel laid up for the winter knows that, with its depth of heavy keel, there is no safer ship sailing the Firth. Every possible danger and emergency has been calculated to a nicety in the construction of the ship. By the same token, hidden away from the gaze of men are pains and necessities which, in the hands of God, may be a man's supreme qualification for preaching the Gospel. Here is an equipment which can be acquired at no university.

> He cannot heal who has not suffered much,
> For only sorrow, sorrow understands.
> They will not come for healing at our touch
> Who have not seen the scars upon our hands.

3

Of the Lord Jesus Christ, William Booth was able to say: "He has had the whole of me." May we lesser men be able to say the same. Consecrate every gift you possess to the preaching of the Gospel—your scholarship, your heritage from a Christian home, your personality. And yield to God's moulding Hands your failure and your contrition, your doubts and your sorrows, and, in the same Hands, nothing you have attained, nothing you have suffered, will ever be lost in the art and practice of your high calling.

CHAPTER III

THE TRAVAIL OF PREPARATION

AMONG the blessings conferred on us by the wireless, there is one that has a special appeal to all who are possessed of any spiritual sensitiveness. Before we plunge into the maelstrom of the day, we listen to four words which carry with them strange, healing benediction: "Lift up your hearts." It is on this intimate note that we would embark on our theme for to-day—Sermon Preparation—for there is a disabling mood which is apt to come down on us with the years which must be conquered before we get under way with our weekly task. It is the mood of doubt, that looks too far ahead, with no glow of expectation, but with the burdened sense of a demand made upon us which we shall never be able to meet. We conceive ourselves as sitting down every week beside some monstrous insatiable machine, which we have to keep feeding, whether we are alert or sluggish, buoyant or bilious. Now there can be no quietude of spirit till this doubting mood is driven out by one that is manlier and wiser. I can remember going, as a young minister, fresh from college, to the experienced man to whom I was assistant and telling him that, having preached four sermons, I had preached my all. The prospect of long years ahead, giving out what was not there to give, filled me, in anticipation, with blank despair. He said, quietly, three words which have often comforted me: "*The manna falls*." Like others who are approaching the close of a long ministry, one can look back and witness with joy that it is of God's fulness we have been receiving, wave after wave of grace, never-failing divine reinforcements coming to our rescue in our human efforts to keep fresh and convincing and abreast of the years. And so, one would say to a younger generation of preachers, "Lift up your hearts." It is not the habit of God to set you, as David did Uriah the Hittite, in the forefront of the battle and then draw off His aid from you, leaving you to your doom. "Lift up your hearts." Not only is God behind you. Comfort yourselves with the thought of all who eagerly await your message. If there be those who will be carpingly critical or drowsily indifferent, there will be far more who will be highly expectant, fervidly anxious to work out in creative living what you have worked in by passionate preaching. The best sermons are those conceived in this climate of glowing hope. "Let your hope be a joy unto you. Lift up your hearts."

In such an atmosphere, then, let us assume the passage selected and the text chosen. If I might speak from my own experience, such as it is, my first advice would be this—clear your desk of everything but your writing pad and your fountain-pen, and for at least two hours consult no white man. I am convinced that the first panic-stricken rush into the arms of the waiting commentators is the death of any originality a man may possess. Allow me here to quote at length words spoken by Dr. Johnson on the study of Shakespeare, which are laden with wisdom for the preacher's approach to the Bible. "Let him who is as yet unacquainted with the powers of Shakespeare and who desires to feel the highest pleasures that the drama can give, read every play from the first scene to the last with utter negligence of all his commentators. When his fancy is on the wing, let it not stop at correction or explanation. Let him read on through brightness or obscurity, integrity or corruption; let him preserve his comprehension of the dialogue and his interest in the fable, and when the pleasures of novelty have ceased, let him attempt exactness and read the commentators." All who have taken the Doctor at his word will agree with him. To allow oneself to be carried on headlong by the rush and swirl of a play like *Macbeth* towards its awesome climax is to know the supreme exhilaration of the study of Shakespeare. The bearing of all this on the task of sermon preparation will be obvious. Without haste, garnering the resources of no one's experience but your own, sit down and listen to what the passage has to say to your own soul. At first the discipline will be well-nigh intolerable. It will be like being thrust out, half-naked, into a cold February morning and, at the end of two hours' lonely wrestling, you may feel you could inscribe the hard-won results on your thumb-nail. My word to you is: "Persevere." In this solitary travail you will be adding cubits to your stature as a preacher and as a man.

Of course, we hasten to the obvious corollary. Having subjected yourself faithfully to this preliminary discipline, you will call in the aid of the saints and the scholars. It is one thing to go through an art gallery alone; it is quite another to be led and instructed by a gifted artist. In the same way, a commentator like Dr. A. C. Bradley will show you a thousand things in Shakespeare you would never have discovered in a lifetime of solitary study.

Of the making of commentaries there is no end. All that one can hope to accomplish in a busy ministry will be to master some of the greatest. I speak to those here whose answer to their country's need in the Services has prevented their achieving a working knowledge of the original tongue of Scripture. With Greek they may have some acquaintance; with Hebrew, none. I was condoling lately, somewhat unnecessarily, it turned out, with a young minister whose war service allowed him to go forward without Hebrew. With a fierce kind of frankness, he told me that rather than face the torment of acquiring it, he would willingly go back to the Navy! In these special circumstances one would say to the young minister: "Buy every modern translation and paraphrase on which you can lay your hands." After all, what are the scholars for? Each minister's library will possess at least half a dozen of the best known. In addition to these, I have found much suggestiveness in Cornish's *St. Paul from the Trenches*, from Dr. Russell Maltby's brief, incomparable paraphrase of the eighth chapter of Romans, also the latest translations of the New Testament Letters, one by the Bishop of London, and another from which I have received great stimulus—*Letters to Young Churches*, by J. B. Phillips. But here I should again refer you to your own professors as sure and competent guides.

To secure the interest of your hearers from the outset I am a strong believer in finding *a succinct and lucid title* for every sermon. When you have clarified your thought and plotted out the trend of your discourse, strive to find some title which, in fewest words, suggests the thought, the whole thought, and nothing but the thought. I would go further and say that you have not clarified your thought *until* you can discover some such arresting title. Much care, we would go on to say, should naturally be given to your opening sentences. You will, of course, practise variety. Now and then you may open with an arresting illustration, but I would make a plea for another method as an alternative. Nothing piques the best kind of curiosity like a brief, pistol-shot opening sentence. Let me give you two examples. The first occurs in a posthumous volume of sermons by that rare spirit, J. K. Thomson. The title of the sermon is "I have kept the Faith." The first sentence is "It was about the only thing Paul had kept." Then follows a moving list of the material sacrifices the apostle had made for Christ's sake and the Gospel's. Take another example. This preacher's text was: "I am determined to know nothing among you save Jesus Christ and Him crucified." The first sentence was: "Once bitten, twice shy." Immediately the preacher proceeded to explain that the method of approach used by St. Paul on Mars' Hill, and used in vain, namely that of seeking to gain a footing for his own revolutionary message by meeting his hearers on their own ground, is here discarded and, without apology or delay, he confronts these questioning Athenians with the stark offence of the Cross. May I go further and ask you to pare your introduction to the bone? Eighty per cent of your hearers are woefully ignorant of the Bible. Condense the findings of the scholars into the fewest words possible and proceed without delay to your explication. Whether the sermon will be the old-fashioned "three-decker" or whether you have mastered the cumulative method of driving home a great spiritual principle by one example after another—that is a matter each man must settle for himself. To those of you who, like myself, have a "melting" for the three heads, see that they really represent three aspects of the main truth, so that they glide into one another. Otherwise, they will be three sermonettes without any logical connection. As I have asked you to look well to your opening words, still more I beseech you to spend much time in wording your closing appeal. This should be simple and heart-felt and, if possible, should be memorised. I had as a member of one of my congregations an elderly doctor, the son of a Disruption minister. He was a hanging judge of a sermon, but his criticisms, offered in the friendliest spirit, were a liberal education. I can still hear him expostulating with me: "Why, oh why, when you had got us all by the heartstrings with a few simple closing words, did you drag in a long, obscure quotation from Robert Browning?" I have never forgotten his protest and I have since tried to be inexorable in the choice of closing sentences, especially in the type of sermon which craves for a verdict. It is not for nothing that Christ's habitual form of words in closing was "He that hath ears to hear, let him hear"; as we would say to-day, "This means *you*." We are told that Queen Victoria used to complain that Mr. Gladstone addressed her as if she were a public meeting. Doubtless the great and good man would sometimes be so carried away with his own eloquence that he became totally oblivious of his audience. Nothing can be further from this than the impact of our Lord on the hearts of His hearers. Men felt themselves taken aside, searched, challenged, smitten, brought to a decision in virtue of which life could never be the same again. Either they made the great refusal and His Face haunted them to their dying day, or they made the great acceptance and every day they lived confirmed their conviction that they had been wise with a wisdom not of this

41

world. One asks wistfully if there is much of this kind of preaching to-day. Over forty years ago two students came up from a provincial town and worshipped for the first time in a great city church. The music was of a standard they had not heard before, and the service became ever more impressive. The sermon was of the old type, massive, deliberate, calm; in the end, piercingly direct and challenging—all the more so because it was wholly without rhetoric. But these two lads walked the long way home to their lodgings, neither uttering a word nor wishing to do so, knowing only that for both of us, to the end of our days, the service would be an ineffaceable memory.

Might I interpolate a plea for omitting, as far as may be, the stereotyped ways of passing from one thought to another? Firstly, secondly, thirdly, should be avoided or submerged. Above all, beware of that mantrap "Finally." The Apostle himself fell into the snare. In the Epistle to the Philippians, you remember, he uses it when he is only halfway through his thought, to start up a totally new subject. Here, in the words of your Professor Tindal, "St. Paul is the father of all preachers who use 'finally, my brethren' as an indication that they have found their second wind!"

Something should also be said on the subject of *variety in preaching*. There are the obvious ways of reaching this desirable end, by following the Christian year, by resolving that, as far as may be, we shall take our hearers through the whole of Scripture and not

42

skip here and there through its pages, choosing texts
that are personally congenial. Such preaching carries
its own Nemesis, and the cure for it is found in loving
the Bible for its own sake, going through it not "lusting
for texts," but for the building up of our own spiritual
life. Nor am I thinking of the obvious and compelling
divisions into which all well-planned preaching will
naturally fall—doctrinal, ethical, pastoral, expository
and evangelistic. I am thinking more of variety in the
choice of texts. This may be a personal idiosyncrasy,
but I find an unfailing interest in trying to discover
suggestive *concatenations of texts*. For this purpose, of
course, the concordance is one's happy hunting-ground,
bringing together so many texts on related themes. It
is a method that has been used by many of our greatest
preachers. Dr. Alexander McLaren, for instance, has
this concatenation: "The wicked hath said, 'I shall
never be moved'." "I said in my prosperity, 'I shall
never be moved'." "Because I have set the Lord ever
before me, I shall never be moved." Legions of
preachers have shamelessly borrowed the late Dr.
George Morrison's triple grouping in a study of de-
generation. "Demas, my fellow-labourer." "Demas."
"Demas hath forsaken me, having loved this present
world." Once, on holiday, I heard an uplifting and
comforting sermon on the phrase "But God." "Man
looketh on the outward appearance, but God looketh
on the heart." "As for you, ye meant evil against me,
but God sent me before you to preserve life. So now

it was not you that sent me hither but God." "Ye were dead in trespasses and sins, but God, who is rich in mercy, hath quickened us together with Christ." Or you may be interested in these two of my own: "Lord, speak to my brother." "Lord, speak to my sister." You may be preaching on the theme "Disappointment —His appointment," where you might take as three stages in St. Paul's education the words "Bithynia, Mysia, Troas." Finally, I recall a most effective sermon taken from the opening verses of three consecutive chapters in Genesis—the seventh, eighth, and ninth. The first may be condensed into three words, "God called Noah"; the second reads, "God remembered Noah"; the last, "God blessed Noah"; three stages in the soul's experience of the grace of God. Do not despise this search for these concatenations of texts as a kind of homiletical jugglery. They can be turned into preaching that is suggestive, arresting, and of real profit. A word in season here on the subject of *outré* texts. There is a period in the education of some young ministers when this amounts to a mania. The veteran golfer, J. H. Taylor, once listened sardonically to two youths describing how they had brought to a fine art two different strokes—in the one case a "slice," in the other a "pull." His one comment was: *What ails ye at the fairway?* Which thing is a parable. The choice of texts that lie far out of the beaten track has its advantages, but should be used in moderation. For one sermon on "Ephraim is a cake not turned" or "Is thy

44

servant a dog?" or "Out came this calf," it were advisable to preach a score on the great immemorial texts like "Come unto me all ye that labour" or "God so loved the world." The *outré* text is the confectionery of preaching. The other is its daily bread.

We pass now to the debated subject of:

*Sermon Illustration*

In certain quarters it has become the habit to disparage the use of this sermonic aid. Years ago Denney, in his sweeping way, told us that quotation and illustration were, in most cases, sheer laziness to think out one's own thought. Now there *are* preachers whose method of sermon preparation seems to be the search for three anecdotes, setting them down like three islands in a homiletical sea, the rest of the sermon consisting in swimming breathlessly from one to the other in the lively hope of coming safely to land. Moreover, if there is one thing a discerning hearer rightly abhors it is, illustrating what, in Charles Lamb's phrase, is "obvious to a sucking babe." There is a delicious commentary on this practice in C. E. Montague's fascinating book, *Disenchantment*, written after the first Great War. It is a picture of "an old Colonel, upright, dutiful, waxen, unintelligent, drawn away by a genuine patriotism from his roses and his croquet, to teach the men of the new army a few of the higher qualities of the old. Too honest a man to pretend that he was not taking all he said in his lecture out of the Army's *Official Manual Infantry Training*, he held the little red book in his hand, read out frankly a sentence at a time from that terse and luminous masterpiece, and proceeded to 'explain' it, while the men gaped at the strange contrast between the thing clearly said in the book, and the same thing plunged into obscurity by the poor Colonel's woolly and faltering verbiage, bringing his laboured jets of darkness to show the way through sunlight, elucidating plainness itself with the tangled clues of his own mind's confusion, like Bardolph —'Accommodated, that is, when a man is, as they say, accommodated, or when a man is being, whereby as may be thought to be accommodated'."

Yet while illustration may be an infuriating superfluity I am still convinced that, skilfully used, it is the most powerful weapon in the preacher's armoury. I would put it in this way. If your congregation were to consist wholly of professors and lecturers or—a more devastating ordeal—of divinity students, I would say eschew altogether the anecdote and the illustration. But if, as is most likely, your people are out with that select category and consist of plain, working folks, what then? I remember a busy Glasgow merchant taking me aside and saying: "If you ministers knew the tension and over-busyness of our working days, and how difficult it is for our tired brains to follow your abstract reasoning, you would not be above a simple, childlike story, now and then"—a reasonable plea from one speaking for the large majority of an average congregation. Let your finding of apt illustrations, then, be an important part of your weekly preparation. No need for me to say "Avoid all those despicable substitutes for your own labour which may be summarily comprehended under the titles 'Tools for Teachers' and 'Plums for Preachers'." Make it a constant joy to discover your own illustrations, from science and literature, from the newspapers, from personal contacts with the so-called common man—if you can find him—from any source in the world that is not pedantic and merely academic. Live with the best literature and be lured into the realms of gold. You will not only fall for the witchery of words and phrases, you will learn to move easily amid the great preoccupations of the human heart, and your resources for illustration will present you with only one problem—what to reject and discard. The older one grows, the slower one is to recommend any book or author to another. The book that sets one man ablaze leaves another cold. We each travel towards a book with our own garnered knowledge of life and with our own temperament and idiosyncrasies. Coleridge was able to say that no day of his life passed without his opening one or another of Shakespeare's plays. We cannot all be Coleridges, but it were a wise purpose, early in our ministry, to resolve that, apart from our theological and devotional reading, we will give our minds, with ever more concentration, to the works of him who is not so much a dramatist as a world. Let me recount a personal experience. My second charge was in a quiet farming district in the south of

Scotland. At the beginning of my first summer I was led to concentrate on the greatest biography in our language, and read, without haste and without rest, Boswell's masterpiece. It was the beginning of an enthralment which has grown with the years. It has resulted in the building up of a Johnsonian library, modest, of course, in extent, but inexhaustible in fertility of illustration and in insight into the human heart. Each of you, I repeat, must find your own enchantment. Such a discipline will save you from all manner of narrowness and unhealthy introspection, and will make your preaching humane, tolerant, rich in understanding of those ever-recurring needs you are to fathom and to satisfy.

# CHAPTER IV

## THE ORDEAL ITSELF

WE now pass to the ordeal of the Lord's Day, when our preparation, our motives and our character come up for judgment. And here let me offer my one original contribution to the subject of effective preaching. I know in advance that, in the case of many of you, my precious seed will fall on stony ground, but that will not deter me from sowing it. I am weighing my words when I say that if there is one habit more than another that has been of value in the art of preaching it is that of *early rising*. I claim no credit for the practice, for I believe just as strongly in going early to bed. It is all a question of capturing for our high task that part of our day when the brain is most alert and the spirit most receptive. Especially on Sunday morning have I found the habit infinitely rewarding. Preaching is, above all other arts, the fruit of a mood, an emerging from an atmosphere. In the rush of the ministry to-day, we must contrive to get our thinking done in the rapidly diminishing intervals between telephone calls—a modern torment which, after long years, I have never been able to bear with Christian resignation. It has blown to the winds more homiletical inspiration than any other device known

4                    49

to man. There are two enemies of great preaching. One is *haste*. The other is *noise*. Readers of Trevelyan's classic life of Macaulay will note with a kind of envy how the latter plotted out the weeks, months and years ahead for the composing of his famous history. The motto for this organised tranquillity of method he found in Chaucer's words:

> There is na workeman
> That can both worken well and hastilie.
> This must be done at leisure, parfaitlie.

Now the tempo of our present-day ministry has been accelerated till the brain reels. We study with a pistol at our heads. Macaulay's example is a counsel of perfection. Still, with the years we learn the art of using every crevice of the time at our disposal. We must beware of self-pity in this connection. After all, we have all the time there is. If we wait for perfect conditions for sermon preparation, we shall have a long wait. We learn to make the most even of a day that is riddled with interruptions. "He that observeth the winds, will not sow. He that regardeth the clouds will not reap." In my early days I had much to learn in this connection. When a sermon of special difficulty or importance was on hand, I would sometimes craftily arrange that my wife and children would spend a day's holiday in the city. Here, one conceived, were the ideal conditions for sermon preparation as described in the hymn "Peace, perfect peace, with loved ones far away"! The experiment was the dismal failure it deserved to be. The silence was funereal, not inspirational. For the comfort of younger men, we older ministers would testify that the art of concentrated thinking and rapid expression grows with the years. Some of our best sermons are born of the highest pressure. When someone doubted the possibility of the unhappy Rev. Dr. Dodd composing a sermon on the eve of his execution, believing that it had a great deal more force in it than anything known to be his, Dr. Johnson answered: "Why should you think so? Depend upon it, sir, when a man knows he is to be hanged in a fortnight, it concentrates the mind wonderfully." And by the same token the ominous and rapid approach of Sunday has a similar quickening effect. To put it at its highest, perhaps it is part of God's loving and merciful plan for us that the weeks that have been overcrowded with urgent visitation are those which may be the prelude to our best sermons. Practical faithfulness brings its own reward, and on these occasions when leisured thinking has been almost impossible, we may receive direct from God a sermon not made with hands. So much for haste. There is a worse evil under the sun, and it is noise. The best kind of preaching is bathed in quietness. Now there is one hour of the week when you are immune from this enemy of mankind. It is six o'clock on Sunday morning. I am not pleading for the impossible conditions in the working ministry that Thomas Carlyle demanded for the composition of his works—the padded room. Even there, we are told, his fastidiousness defeated itself for he said it was not the actual crowing of the cock that drove him half crazy: it was the keyed-up *waiting for the next cock-crow*. These three precious hours on Sunday morning, undistracted by noisy invasions, bring certain inestimable benefits. The first is, that the stillness brings down on the spirit the dews of God's presence. "Enter into thy chamber and shut the door and pray to thy Father Who seeth in secret"—and in faring forth, strangely empowered and undergirded, God will reward you openly. As to the content of such prayer-discipline, that will be obvious to every spiritual mind—the laying bare before the All-seeing Eye of our motives in preaching, the resolute turning of our gaze from the earthen vessel to the precious treasure it contains, the prayer that the word to be spoken in God's name may fall on receptive hearts, the holding of God to His promise that He will make His strength perfect in our weakness, above all for the descent of the Holy Ghost, for that pure Presence, in which all manner of insincerity, affectation and unreality shall shrivel and perish—so that there may enter into the coming service nothing that defileth or maketh a lie. I ask you, can you conceive of any duty or privilege more likely than this to call down the divine blessing on the preaching of the word? "Hast thou commanded the morning?" Here is a word either of haunting reproach or of wondrous inner replenishing for our great task of proclaiming the Gospel of Jesus Christ, the Son of God.

On the second benefit of capturing for God the early hours of His own day, I shall only, in the meantime, say this. In my own case it has gone a long way towards solving the question of public prayer, "extempore" or written and read. Many of you will have already settled this vexed question by resolving to read all your prayers, after the most careful preparation. Here no man would dictate to others. For myself, the writing and reading of public prayer is wholly unnatural. I find that two or three hours of quiet premonitory brooding on the coming prayers, on the thought and climate—not on the language, make me believe that if the spirit is sincerely prepared, the appropriate word will seldom be missing. This habit begets a warmth and spontaneity in prayer which I, at least, could never achieve in the read prayer. If you cling to your belief in writing and reading your prayers, let me give you one word of counsel. I remember, on holiday, hearing a minister conduct a service. The sermon was able and helpful, but the devotions were quite unworthy of it. One had the feeling—nay, the certainty, that just before he had left his manse the preacher had opened a deep drawer containing his accumulation of written prayers, and pounced on the first that came to hand. Again and again, perhaps because he could not make out his own handwriting, he stumbled and had to return to the beginning of a sentence. The effect was simply shocking. Nothing could have been more soul-less. If, then, you believe in written prayers, see that you live into them before you come to the pulpit. Otherwise, they will be as stale as the remainder biscuit.

And so we pass from the study to the vestry, where you will wish to have a good conscience regarding certain things which seem obvious but, cumulatively, can greatly affect the dignity and beauty of the service. You will arrive in ample time. You will have your Order of Service meticulously arranged, your intimations fully written out, the Scripture passages carefully marked—above all, you will insist on fifteen minutes perfect privacy before entering the pulpit, no matter how important be the person to whom you may give offence. Do not be above a reminder of these obvious things. I have seen too many services, conducted by most able preachers, well-nigh ruined because they considered them trivial.

Concerning the Order of Service, each man will claim for himself a large liberty and, in passing, it is only courteous to a visiting minister in sending him your Order of Service to tell him it is to be "his guide and not his chain." As regards the priority of the two main prayers, this has been debated with what seems to me unnecessary heat. We are each entitled to settle the question for ourselves. Personally, I devote the first wholly to Thanksgiving; the other to Confession and Intercession. I would dwell on one special emphasis in the case of the prayer of Confession. It is here that one has one's chief hesitations regarding the writing and reading of prayers. To me, nothing seems more unreal, especially in the case of a young minister, than a prayer of confession with a lengthy list of sins and failures, carefully catalogued and deftly worded yet somehow giving the impression of a literary effort rather than a heartfelt cry for deliverance. To my mind this prayer should be brief, fervent, almost ejaculatory. Moreover, let us remember our priestly office and, taking high ground, never fail in the proclamation of God's absolution, the terms, of course, being expressed in various ways. I submit that we Protestants should be able, in Christ's name, to offer to penitent hearts all the benefits of the Roman confessional with none of its abuses. You are aware that it is one of the rules of the Catholic confessional that the penitent pledges himself never to reopen what once has been confessed, either with his confessor or anyone else. Why should not we of the Protestant faith be able to direct contrite souls to the exulting assurance that their sins are buried in the deep sea of God's forgetting and forgiving love, and that they pass from the service with the gladness of pardon, men and women free to choose the better part and to be children of the light and the day? If, in this prayer of confession, we are enabled, under God, to bring such full enfranchisement to a single heart, we have accomplished a work that is truly great. Here you will learn to judge your congregation by its most sensitive spirits, believing that for one who

is "not worrying about his sins" there are three who
are aching for the calm of sin forgiven. Regarding the
prayer of Intercession, I would say only this. I believe
in closing it with a brief silence unto God, the period
being introduced by such a sentence as, "O Thou
who knowest how no one voice can interpret the needs
of so many, hear us as we bring to Thee in the stillness,
our secret and unspeakable prayers for others and for
ourselves," the period being brought to a close with
the request that God may answer these according to
His wisdom and His love.

In speaking of the devotional service, one can record
one's pleasure in the services of to-day compared with
those of one's early days in the ministry. Thank God
we hear no more that dreadful word "preliminaries".
The increased emphasis and instruction in the liturgical
has awakened a growing generation of ministers to the
power and beauty of true worship. One wonders, in
fact, if we are not in danger of going to the other
extreme, till the sermon becomes of secondary importance. That, of course, were sheer apostasy. However,
the redressing of the balance was long overdue. It is
good to feel that the young preachers of to-day know
that long before the first word of the sermon is uttered
its success or failure has been decided by the preparation, painstaking or otherwise, of the devotions of the
sanctuary. May I add that the studied preparation of
pulpit prayer—and just as carefully—of the reading of
the Scripture has one most comforting adjunct? On

the rare occasions on which we listen to another minister, we are relieved to find that the desperate sense of carrying the whole service on one's own shoulders is largely unnecessary. We learn, as I have just said, that long before the sermon begins a tidal wave of devotion and hallowed song has flooded the hearts of every true worshipper, and that the seed falls on soil wonderfully watered by God's Holy Spirit. This thought should give us the calmness, the restraint, the quiet confidence and holy expectancy that should always go with true preaching. Here, one would say in passing, emerges the supreme importance of a close and happy collaboration with one's organist and choir. The presence or absence of such co-operation is swift to be noted by the discerning hearer.

From the devotional service we pass to a brief word on *sermon delivery*. In this matter of voice production, no man can advise another. We have the voice God has given us and no other, and we must resolve by every means and with persevering patience to make it the disciplined servant of our divine message. If there is one word I would utter it would be this. There are many ways of being monotonous, and most of us have been guilty of them all. But there is none so common, and certainly none so irritating, as the monotony of earnestness. There are preachers whose one idea in the matter seems to be that "the Kingdom of Heaven suffereth violence and the violent take it by force." From the first syllable of the sermon till the last they turn on full blast. The result is that their very earnestness defeats itself. There is nothing more intriguing and rewarding than learning the art of "light and shade" in preaching, how to begin quietly and deliberately, when, and by what gradual stages, to rise to the full voice, the use of the effective pause, even the instinctive whisper, and the vibrating, subdued restraint of the final appeal. A man must devise his own way of entering into what he is thinking and saying in a sermon. For this, there is no better way than declaiming his sermon aloud in his study and watching the effect on his own heart. The sermon that rings true in emotion and expression in the privacy of his own chamber, will find its way home to other hearts in the warm glow of the sanctuary.

We pass to the subject of:

*Methods of Sermon Delivery*

Obviously, one who reads every word of his sermon misses the undoubted inspiration of responsive faces. On the other hand, the preacher who plumes himself on being able to preach without a scrap of paper is in a much more parlous situation. The longer one is in the ministry and subject to its desperate strain on the memory, the more one refuses to burden it with superfluous lumber. The man who preaches without notes must either commit his quotations and illustrations to memory or do without these altogether. Surely the *via media* at once suggests itself—the use of fairly copious notes, with a synopsis of the quotations and illustrations, so that we can still look our audience in the face. All this, of course, may be controversial. I have heard preachers who could read every word with perfect success, expressing the thought beautifully, without being in the least tied to the paper. Only once did I hear a minister who deeply moved me and who used not a single note. In his case, he was a really distinguished preacher, with an original gift of words and possessed of an amazing memory. Even so, truth to tell, he was doubtless delivering a sermon he had used again and again. Especially would I implore young ministers to resist the temptation, for temptation it is, to preach without notes. I listened but lately to a shrewd doctor delivering himself of a pent-up load of irritation against the good minister to whom he strove to be loyal, because of the preacher's insufferable repetitions which would have been unnecessary had he known he was the last man in the world who should have dispensed with paper. My own conviction is that only one man in a hundred can preach without notes. If that one man be here, will he do me a special favour? Will he resist, like a temptation of the Evil One, the practice of giving out his text and then ostentatiously closing his Bible? Vanity and egotism are, in nearly every case, behind this irritating habit, and verily they have their reward. If you preach without notes, *keep the Bible open*. One is reminded here of the aggressive lady who twitted the poet Addison with his lack of conversational gifts. "Madam," he replied, "I have

59

only ninepence in ready money, but I can draw for a thousand pounds." The moral for the extempore preacher is obvious. The discerning hearer will always be compensated for the speaker's penury by the mere sight of the open Bible. Here, at least, is God's Word, which is "God's plenty".

A word on *personality* in the pulpit. The true preacher is totally oblivious of himself. A man should never be in the least apologetic about his personality, though he should always be open to the kindly criticism of those who could help him to shear away his eccentricities. One of the greatest sermons on the greatest of subjects that I ever heard was by the late Professor W. P. Paterson, on "The Forgiveness of Sins." Who that ever listened to him—the scholarly mind glowing with the passion of the Evangel—could forget the sight of a personality all its own, utterly lost in his theme, giving to every thought a strange combination of virility and winsomeness? But who would for a moment have thought of imitating the Professor's mannerisms and quaint postures? Here, as everywhere, the word is, "Be yourself and no other."

A question that arises is, how far is it wise, or even legitimate, to read other people's sermons—even the greatest? It will be clear that the practice has its uses and abuses. As regards training in style and composition, its benefits are obvious. We live in a preaching age, when the tendency is all towards the discarding of every redundant word, towards the style that is the everyday language of our hearers. Lest we go too far in this direction, so that our diction tends to degenerate into cheapness or even slang, it were good to sit down, now and then, and study the sermons of a former generation when the language was much more ornate and sonorous. Personally, I enjoy the discipline of studying carefully the sermons of such a master as Principal John Caird. There is a rich flow, a captivating eloquence in these pages that, in themselves, bear a great spiritual uplift, all the more that this eloquence is employed towards the most practical ends, as in his truly great sermon, "Religion in Common Life." For myself, I have often spent a whole forenoon studying the language and brooding on the austere thought of a single sermon by James Martineau. It is like walking down the aisles of a venerable cathedral. Present-day sermons, I imagine, should be read almost wholly for the sake of our own devotional life. It is the supreme deprivation of the ministry that we ministers hear the Gospel only through our own lips and from our own sermons. Needless to say, we should take every opportunity of hearing the outstanding preachers of to-day. I myself have travelled long distances and given up two week-ends of my summer holidays for such rare opportunities, and the privilege has been enhanced when one has been able to listen to the best preachers outside one's own denomination.

On the abuses of reading other people's sermons it is scarcely necessary to say more than a few words. It is one thing to borrow a kindling from another man's sermons, and when anyone is daring enough to publish a book of sermons he must expect them to become public property. It is quite another thing to make an illegitimate use of them and to risk the most discreditable of all charges. It is told that the late Professor Saintsbury was one day announcing the results of an essay competition on the works of Thomas Carlyle. One student had borrowed shamelessly from Professor Nichol's book on Carlyle, in the English Men of Letters Series. Said Professor Saintsbury: "On this occasion I am giving the first place to the second best essay. The best is that by Professor Nichol, handed in by Mr. So-and-so." I have skirted the unsavoury subject of plagiarism in a lightish vein. The one way to keep ourselves from the faintest suspicion of it is to preserve a rigorous scrupulousness, acknowledging frankly the source of everything we borrow. Moreover, the man whose shelves are lined with other men's sermons is a traitor to that measure of originality, however meagre, with which God has endowed him.

Let me close this lecture with an austere repetition of two thoughts. "The test of any vocation is the love of the drudgery it involves"; and the other is like unto it: "All the travail of sermon preparation is repaid in the pulpit with mathematical exactitude." Failure and success in preaching point the same obvious lesson. I can remember, as a young student, listening to what must have been the most amazing opening to any sermon ever preached. The minister was a dear old man, and he obviously knew his people familiarly. But on this occasion, it seemed to me, he strained their loyalty to breaking-point. He began naively and tentatively, like a man testing with his foot a rotten plank. "I have often found that some of my best holidays have been those for which I have planned nothing, but have simply stepped out of my manse door and followed where my feet chose to carry me. I propose to do much the same with this text." I draw a veil over the sequel! The sermon was indeed a mystery tour. Dean Inge has a caustic word here. He uses it in another connection, but its application to our pulpit preparation—or want of it—will not be lost. "The student who imagines he can play the slacker for months before an important examination is made to learn that God is on the side of the examiners."

With high seriousness in our sacred calling, I would warm your hearts to the contrary experience. If there be a greater joy on earth than to stand before an expectant congregation, purified by earnest prayer and clean motives, warmed by the one passion of preaching God's redeeming love, I, for one, have yet to hear of it. It is a joy open to every man who is prepared to pay the price. You are all familiar with Bunyan's famous picture of the consecrated preacher "with the best of books in his hand and the world behind his back." I close with one less familiar but, to my mind, no less impressive. Of John Donne these words were written by his friend, Izaac Walton: "He preached the word so as showed his own heart was possest with those very thoughts and joyes he laboured to distill into others, a Preacher in earnest, weeping sometimes *for* his Auditory, sometimes *with* them, always preaching to himself like an angel *from* a cloud but *in* none, carrying some as St. Paul did, to heaven in holy raptures, and enticing others by a sacred art and courtship to amend their lives; here picturing a vice so as to make it ugly to those that practised it, and a vertue so as to make it beloved by those who loved it not, all this with a most particular grace and an unexpressible addition of comeliness."

CHAPTER V

## THE MINISTER'S DEVOTIONAL LIFE

ANY treatment of this subject must avoid two
extremes. The first is the dangerous tendency to
make the devotional life an end in itself. At the risk of
being misunderstood, one might say that there is no
reputation that carries greater danger than that of
being "a minister of outstanding devotional gifts". The
stern truth is that along with this endowment may go
a spirit that shrinks from the drudgery that makes up
most of our working career. To quote a somewhat
brutal but salutary saying, "There are Christians so
heavenly-minded that they are of no earthly use."
Again, an unbalanced devotionalism may be accom-
panied by what amounts to contempt of that intellectual travail by which alone we can keep abreast of
modern thinking. Far more serious than either consideration is another which not even the surest of us
may ignore. The man who has not discovered that
there is within him but a thin film between the emotional and the sensual may one day be stabbed broad
awake to the need of eternal vigilance in that moral
warfare to which all of us, as ministers and as men, are
for ever conscript.

The other side of all this will be obvious. It is the

5

perilous supposition that if we are putting the last ounce of energy into practical service, our devotional life can take care of itself. Far too much has been made of the well-known story of Wilberforce and the lady who asked him whether, amid his multifarious duties on behalf of the slave, he was not neglecting his own soul. The reply was: "Madam, I forgot I had a soul." But the lady was not wholly wrong. The hectic, over-driven, almost embittered spirit that can be generated by the exactions of the ministry needs a continuous infiltration of the winds of Heaven. We must learn, wisely and frequently, to come apart and rest awhile. "A man is not defrauding his employer when he pauses to whet his scythe."

Having entered this caveat let us consider our devotional life in its relation to God, to others, and to ourselves.

*Growing into God*

Every young ordinand, ere he kneels for the laying on of hands, is asked a question which not even the oldest minister present can hear without a clutch at the throat. "Are not zeal for the glory of God, love to the Lord Jesus Christ, and a desire for the salvation of men, so far as you know your own heart, your great motives and chief inducements to enter into the office of the Holy Ministry?"

Words like these are a consuming fire. Every minister, as he values his own soul, will return to them, again and again, as to "the altar that he had made there at the first." How is this first purity of consecration to be retained amid the wear and tear, the disillusionment with others and with oneself, that come upon us so insidiously with the testing years? The answer is not far to seek. It lies in an ever-deepening sense of God. In that fascinating autobiography, *So Far*, by W. J. Brown, the writer, on one page, rises suddenly above caustic criticism of some of his own party to unbounded eulogy of one who was patently a man apart. Of the late Robert Smillie, he says: "He impressed me as a man whose life was overshadowed by the eternal and whose life was lived under other eyes than those of his fellow-men. The values saturating him derived beyond time and lent to his utterances a quality which was difficult to define but most potent to feel." Herein lies the secret of all spiritual power. To live in this climate is to live in a world where the meaner passions shrivel and die. The man who has an awesome sense of God, the man who knows that what other men call their privacy is a region that lies forever in the white light of the divine scrutiny, is delivered, once for all, from such a vice as jealousy. The man in whose thought and prayer God ever looms greater knows that in the ministry no man is his competitor. With perfect humility he believes that no other can fill his particular niche in the economy of God. The man who cannot sincerely rejoice in another man's gifts has no call to the ministry. Neither has he who has not learned, with his two talents, to work loyally with him who has five. Moreover, it cannot be said too strongly that a growing sense of God is the only antidote to that inordinate love of praise and publicity which, in some men, "eateth as doth a canker."

Again, this developing sense of God saves a man from the spiritual debility that so often follows on the long tension of the ministerial calling. It is the subtle temptation to become cynical about our vocation, the feeling that we have been stampeded by a youthful emotion into a career for which we afterwards find ourselves to be temperamentally unsuited. There are few of us who are not visited by these revulsions and there are those who succumb to them altogether. A minister must learn, humbly and courageously, to take himself for better or worse. In these moods he must fall back on his sense of God—the compassionate, understanding, merciful God who must have known what He was doing when He chose men like us and must have anticipated the crises of our career when we would need Him most. In this connection a still scene from Hardy's *Woodlanders* comes to mind. Giles Winterbourne is planting young fir trees on a cold wintry morning. "His fingers were endowed with a gentle, conjuring touch in spreading the roots of each little tree, resulting in a sort of caress under which the delicate fibres all laid themselves out in their own proper direction for growth. He put most of these roots towards the south-west, for, he said, in forty years' time when some great gale is blowing from that quarter, the trees will require the strongest holdfast on that side to stand against it and not fall."

The longer we are in the ministry, the surer we become that the same wonderful prevision of our coming necessities has been in the loving heart of God, concerning us. "When some great gale is blowing," He has provided for us His own miraculous "holdfast". Such are the ways of Him "Who never goes back on His call." Towards this most enviable possession, then, should be directed all the hidden endeavour of our devotional life. "Hidden" endeavour is said advisedly. To take oneself seriously and be for ever obtruding our seriousness is the way to all priggishness. To take oneself seriously and keep down the iron lids is the pathway to all spirituality. For this is the paradox of it—that in the end such a quest cannot be hid. There is no limit to the influence of a man of whom it can be said without unreality:

> His one thought was God.
> In that one thought he abode,
> Forever in that thought more deeply sinking.

### Reaching Out to Others

There is also the aspect of our devotional life which turns towards others, towards those whom God has given us to guide. Among the cataclysmic changes wrought in the mind of St. Paul by the Damascus-road experience, he himself underlines one—"Henceforth I know no man after the flesh." In other words, "from now on all the distinctions that play so great a part in the eyes of the world—rank, wealth, learning, prestige or immunity of any kind—for me these have ceased to exist. Henceforth every man is 'a man for whom Christ died,' a person in whose inner life is going on an intense spiritual drama, a conflict between good and evil from which there is no discharge. Henceforth the one effort of my ministry is to be directed to the fanning of the divine flame."

Only by constantly striving to maintain towards our members some such truly spiritual attitude shall we be saved from some of the most subtle snares of our calling. If we descend from it, we may awake to find ourselves quite shamelessly visiting only those of our members who are personally congenial. This is one of the spheres in our calling where we are our own masters, and woe be to us if we play fast and loose with our liberty. There is a kind of treachery to Christ here which brings its own Nemesis. Some day, by the side of a coffin, it may be, we may make the startling discovery that we have had a saint of God in our congregation and have never known it. Hard as it is to maintain this ideal, for special circumstances, trouble or co-operation in congregational work, may bring us closer to some of our members than others, we must strive and pray that our supreme interest in our people may be a spiritual one. We must ask God to give us an ever-enlarging interest in and love for human character, its baffling intricacies, its mingled strength and weakness, its doublings and evasions, its latent heroisms, its hidden sackcloth, its inarticulate longings. By such a discipline of prayer only shall we come to see that behind every façade, beneath every mask of pride, intellectual complacency or worldly security, there is a nature hungering for the living God, and that in the Gospel we have that which makes all men akin and is His last satisfying word to the heart of man.

There is another peril which we must "pray out of our lives". It is the danger of mistaking personal popularity for ministerial success. The ministry is full of the kindly humanities. There is possibly no other profession, unless it be the medical, that generates such warm friendships. We touch people at the most intimate places in their lives—at the happy wedding feast, at the coming of a little child, at the last parting. In such conditions friendship grows to fine fruition. But it is quite possible to be personally acceptable to our people and to fail miserably in that which is the very *raison d'être* of our calling. The very pleasantness of such conditions ought to convey to us a hint of their danger. Pascal has austere words to say on the peril of becoming usurpers of the place of Christ in the affections of our people. It is so easy for a man to congratulate himself on being "a good mixer". There are too many of our members who seem to consider that this is the only reason for a man being in the ministry, and, as if in answer to this clamour, the back-slapping, hail-fellow-well-met parson is ever with us. Let it be a part of our devotional discipline to aim at an influence deeper far and more abiding. A good man once said to the writer on his entering the ministry: "Take Christ with you into the homes of your people and they will take you along with Him." That is the true order, whether the sequel follows or not.

Perhaps the secret of a wise bearing towards all our fellow men, of all classes and temperaments, can only be acquired when we allow our sense of God to regulate our relation to men. There are words of Tagore, the Indian mystic, in this connection which are profoundly moving. "Be not ashamed, my brothers, to stand before the proud and the powerful in your white robes of simpleness. Let your crown be of humility, your freedom the freedom of the soul. Build God's throne daily on the ample bareness of your poverty and know that what is huge is not great and pride is not ever-lasting."

These things having been said, one goes on to speak of the wide field of intercessory prayer that opens out before us as we consider the spiritual needs of our people. A large part of our devotional life will consist in laying before God their multifarious problems and necessities. It is our duty and privilege to share the crises of trouble that come to all. People will often forget the most impressive sermon we have it in us to preach. They will never forget our standing by them in a great sadness. Their very gratitude will often put us to shame. There are certain qualities of mind and heart for which we ought to pray if we would fulfil this priestly office. There is a refinement of tact and grace that comes only of prayer, of understanding, of our own knowledge of suffering. Of Victor Hugo's saintly Bishop Bienvenu, he says: "He understood how to sit down and hold his peace beside the man who had lost the wife of his love, of the mother who had lost her child. As he knew the moment for speech, he knew also the moment for silence." Along with this delicacy of approach we must pray for the gift of the concentration of our sympathy. One of the busiest of city dentists was once asked how he managed to do his work with such calm efficiency when he knew that the adjoining room was crowded with people awaiting his attention. His reply was, *"I have only one patient."* We must show—and this without insincerity—that the person we are trying to help is the one person in the world we are interested in. Without in the least contradicting all this, we must pray for the power of wisely conserving our sympathy. Jane Austen's *Emma* has a saying that sounds harsh, but is only applied commonsense. "I hope it may be allowed that if compassion has produced exertion and relief to the sufferers, it has done all that is truly important. If we feel for the wretched enough to do all we can for them, the rest is empty sympathy, only distressing to ourselves." This saying is quoted because it redresses the balance between an overwrought sympathy and sheer callousness. The deeper an individual is immersed in any Slough of Despond, the more sure we must be to keep on firm ground to help him out. There are limits to our capacities for sympathy. No man could bear the accumulated sorrows of seven or eight hundred people and keep his sanity. We must pray for the power both to give ourselves and yet to conserve ourselves. By prayer and experience we learn to do both.

## Disciplining Ourselves

In no other calling is a man so utterly his own master as in ours. With body and mind, with time and money, we can do what we like. Here we "sink or swim". All this points to a desperate need of some dominant authority. Ours must be the best kind of discipline—a discipline imposed from within. How then is our devotional life to minister to our all-round efficiency?

Let it be stated frankly, though it may sound like a truism, that there is no greater service we can prayerfully offer to God and man than the care and consecration of our own bodies. One is saddened by one tale after another of ministerial breakdown—involving long periods of absence from duty that are infinitely depressing to the invalid himself and a severe strain on the loyalty of his congregation. Let us make this matter of our physical well-being an affair of wise planning and prayerful concern. Otherwise we enter our pulpits the most jaded person in our congregation and radiate anything but the spirit of those who in

Christ are more than conquerors. It is not too much to say that in the case of the average minister our bodily health is largely in our own keeping. How often we are rebuked by the amazing response, the wonderful powers of recuperation the body provides to those who give it its vital place in the economy of the spirit. Our ideal should be:

> Thy body at its best,
> How far can that project thy soul on its lone way?

Let not the minister with the devotional gift think he is above this caution. No man needs it more.

Then we must call in God's help in the management of our time. This is an aspect of our work which tends to reduce us to despair and to chronic bitterness. The pace of the modern ministry has become exasperating. We do our thinking and our praying in the rapidly diminishing intervals between telephone calls. Not even the most considerate of our members can enter into our difficulties here. How is it possible in the whirl of things to maintain a background of quietness?

Perhaps it helps us to remember that the Christian ministry never could be run to a schedule and never will. What "the natural man" in us would consider an irritating interruption may prove to an experienced minister the greatest spiritual opportunity of his day. It gives a new complexion to much of the drudgery and the interruption of the ministry to say concerning it, "This also is for the Kingdom of God." But we must pray to be enlightened of God as to what claims on our time must be given priority. We are apt to be besieged by one earnest person after another, with one society to represent or one cause to support, who knows nothing of the endless calls of our own congregation. Having carefully and prayerfully settled our priorities, let us have the courage to hold to them. That will cause offence. Better that than reducing our life to utter chaos and giving offence to God. He alone knoweth our frame—our capacities and our limitations. Let that suffice.

One yearning haunts the heart of every earnest minister in these overcrowded days. It arises out of the necessity of keeping our own souls. Neglect of this leads to the last irony of the ministerial calling—the days shattered into fragments with no great calming thought of God to give them some kind of unity and plan. Come what may, we must at all costs preserve one portion of the day sacrosanct. Surely there is no time like its beginning. "Hast thou commanded the morning?" is a word either of haunting reproach or of wonderful daily, divine replenishing. To anticipate the day that lies ahead, to frame it in the wise, loving superintendence of a Gracious God is to fare forth strangely guided and strangely girded. To plunge into the maelstrom of the day trusting to chance impulses in ourselves and favouring conditions outside of us is to presume we can do God's work without God, and there is no presumption greater than that.

Again, one often wonders if for our own soul's sake we make enough of another source of spiritual refreshment. I mean the inspiration that comes from warm, intimate, ministerial comradeship. It is no small part of the travail of the ministry that we seldom hear the Gospel but from our own lips. Here, surely, is a great impoverishment. "My Gospel" can never be "The Gospel of Jesus Christ, the Son of God." The one is a tiny creek. The other is the boundless sea. The writer will never forget the impression made upon him when he hurried to offer his condolence to a close friend in the ministry, who had just lost his brilliant, beloved son in the Royal Air Force. "I have no minister," he cried; "sit down and be my minister." Not only in a devastating sorrow, but in the wear and tear of the common day do we cry out for the comfort for ourselves which we mediate to others. There is no lonelier calling on earth than that of a Christian minister. Thank God for the two or three men to whom we can go when our own light burns low, and never without the rekindling of the heavenly flame.

*Devotional Reading*

The older one grows, the slower one is to recommend any book to another. The book that sets one man ablaze leaves another cold. We each travel towards a book with our own garnered knowledge of life. If this is true of general literature, it is ten times true of devotional reading. Of course, there will be a large measure of general agreement. Not for nothing have generations of Christian folks gathered round the great classics of the soul, as round some deep, cool well of water on their long, dusty pilgrimage. Is it superfluous to mention the Bible itself as the supreme source of devotional inspiration? This is a favourite emphasis of Dr. Alexander Whyte in the instruction of his students —to read the Bible not "lusting for texts", but to allow it to make its own impression on the waiting mind and heart. A personal plan is to begin the day reading that inspired compilation, *Daily Readings from Moffatt's Translation of the Bible*. It never fails to provide some kindling thought with which to face the day—and, one may add, with apologies to Dr. Whyte, it seldom fails in homiletical suggestion as the Sunday looms ahead! Or need one mention the English Prayer Book, especially in its ineffably beautiful collects? Well may Robertson of Brighton exclaim of the loveliest of them all: "Strange and magical is the power of that collect wherein we pray to God 'Who alone canst order the unruly wills and affections of sinful men' to grant unto His people that they may love the thing which He commands, and desire that which He promises: that so, among the sundry and manifold changes of the world, our hearts may surely there be fixed, where true joys are to be found."

Our devotional library should be a small one. To try to assimilate the vast collection of the classics of devotion is as foolish as it is unattainable. Just as we each have in our libraries "a bookshelf by the fire" for the few books that really mould us, so in the wide range of devotional literature each of us must find what is for ourselves alone. Following out this thought there may be gratefully quoted a word of sage counsel from the late Principal W. M. Macgregor. It was on the vital necessity of "correcting our bias". As one who is no stranger to the peril of allowing one's devotional life to become an end in itself, the present writer has found the necessary corrective (others may find theirs elsewhere) in the discipline of reading such books as James Martineau's *Endeavours after the Christian Life*, or his *Hours of Thought*. The prevailing *motif* in these austere pages is, "He that doeth the will shall know of the doctrine." It is good, for instance, to awake oneself out of a reverie of devotionalism by a sharp challenge such as this: "No one can have a true idea of right until he does it: any genuine reverence for it, until he does it often and with cost; any peace ineffable in it, until he does it always and with alacrity."

But one would not close on a negative note. The best devotional books "come our way". We do not seek them out. They come, like our best friendships, into our lives with a strange timeliness. In the hope that a few others may share gratitude to God, let but two of these be mentioned. Again and again one can turn to the first six chapters of Dean Church's engrossing *History of the Oxford Movement*. To read these—and re-read them—is to be admitted into a circle of

79

men who dwelt in the innermost sanctuary of God, and to stir within the heart a quenchless craving for spirituality—though the craving may be "the desire of the moth for the star". Here were men "for whom religion was the most awful and personal thing on earth", "who hated show and mistrusted excitement", who evinced "a deep reality of devoutness which it was their great and habitual effort to keep hidden", who displayed "a strong depreciation of mere intellect, compared with the less showy excellences of faithfulness to conscience and duty, and a horror and hatred of everything that seemed like display or the desire of applause or immediate effect." To listen to these men is "to wish myself among them".

To mention one last influence among many, it may be asked if any book has been published in the last few years which breathes such a spirit of inwardness and mysticism as Thomas P. Kelly's *Testament of Devotion*. The air is rarified and the teaching of the book must be harnessed instantaneously to practical service. For pregnant phrasing, piercing appeal, and stark realism, the book is a purification. But here one must cease, once more remembering that God comes to each of us "down His own secret stair".

CHAPTER VI

# THE HINTERLAND

THIS lecture will be largely devoted to the truism
that a man's preaching will never rise higher than
the level of his character. To have won the battle of
one's own soul is half the battle in winning the souls
of others. The first aspect of this contention is one
we cannot learn too early. It is that—*Character and
Reputation are not synonymous.*

In his inimitable *Life of Charles Lamb*, E. V. Lucas
says that one trait of Elia's character which was instinct
in every line he wrote, was his horror of being thought
a better man than he really was. It is a healthy horror,
and one that every true minister ought to pray for as
for a spiritual antiseptic. The fact that, in public, we
are continually using the language of religion is apt to
bring us a reputation for spirituality that may be quite
fictitious. Unless we keep this peril ever before us, we
can fall into the worst kind of self-deception. Something must happen within us, whereby the word
"reputation" fades for ever out of our concern and
out of our vocabulary. There are circles, to be rigidly
eschewed, where ministers are labelled according to
their scholarship, their eloquence, their personality,
their piety. Dr. Jowett once related that, when he was

minister of Fifth Avenue Church, in New York, it was his custom to take a walk in Central Park. He used to turn homewards at a certain plot of ground. Here, one February day, he saw a large bush on which a tin label was swaying in the wind. Being preoccupied with his own thoughts, he gave it no more than a cursory glance. But, coming back on a day in April, the bush thrust itself on his attention. It was now loaded with the loveliest purple blossom. It was only then that he took the trouble to examine the label and read its scientific name. And by the same token the various reputations attached to men of our calling mean little to the spiritually discerning. But the bloom of a life that is obviously rooted in God will never fail to make its impression even on the most critical outsider.

Again, and this for sheer sincerity's sake, we must for ever strive to keep an even balance between the *practical* and the *devotional*. The ceaseless whirl which is the modern ministry tends to destroy the possibility of possessing our own souls in tranquillity. Lord Morley has a striking passage in which he deals with a certain fundamental defect in the writings of Macaulay. After doing justice to the historian's gift of a picturesque and vivid style, he proceeds: "We can picture Macaulay talking, or making a speech in the House of Commons, or buried in a book, or scouring his library for references, or covering his foolscap with dashing periods, or accentuating his sentences and barbing his phrases, but can anyone think of him as *meditating*, as

82

being possessed, for so much as ten minutes, by *that spirit of inwardness* which is the hallmark of the Kings and Princes of Literature?" Substitute the career of the minister for that of the writer, and we have, in these sentences, a flashlight on the superficiality and ineffectiveness of much of our service for God's Kingdom. Yet when this "spirit of inwardness" is blended with tireless practical service, it makes an irresistible combination. It is the explanation of the strange attractiveness of some men's character and preaching. In a thousand ways, what we are prevails over what we say. This has been noted in the case of two great contemporaries, Whately and Newman. "Whately", we are told, "required to bring to the mind of his listeners the clearest intellectual demonstration before he could lead them, whereas they were moved by anything Newman said, from the mere fact that it was he who said it." We must pray, then, for this "spirit of inwardness", that we may "take root downward that we may bear fruit upward." Here alone shall we find the resources that will carry us through the long years. The late Principal Cairns once drew a distinction between two kinds of Christians which is vitally applicable in the ministry. The first, he said, seem to live, as a nation is forced to live during a coal strike, on the bings at the pithead. The second are drawing regularly from the inexhaustible depths of the earth beneath. Sooner or later the difference will assert itself in our preaching as also in our lives.

Now, of course, this cultivation of "the spirit of inwardness" has its obvious peril—unhealthy introspection. This is a very frequent over-emphasis in certain temperaments, and we must strive continually to redress the balance. There is a pseudo-spirituality which is above soiling itself with common things. The late W. L. Watkinson once deftly depicted it in a sardonic sentence. "We all know the saintly sister who can sit for hours by the fire, talking eagerly of entire sanctification, *with a week's ashes lying in her grate!*" If our minds have a dangerously introspective bias, we need this caustic warning. Our difficulty lies in the fact that to understand the hearts of others we must be making continual incursions into our own. But if we allow ourselves to be unduly preoccupied with our own hearts, our prayer life can degenerate into a pitiful Narcissism. To keep the balance true, we must study our Lord's perfect example here as elsewhere. For Him, prayer was never allowed to become an emotional indulgence. It was the girding of His loins for a journey, the trimming of His lamp for the darkness, the putting on of His armour for the battle. We must guard against a morbid and hypersensitive interest in our own character. There are several symptoms of this defect. One is the inability to face obvious and clamant duty till we have put all our motives under a painful and prolonged scrutiny. Another is the shivering fear of criticism, the antidote to which is supplied by the stinging sentence: "To avoid criticism, do nothing, say nothing, be nothing." This strained over-scrupulosity about motives, this inability to face up to the ordinary challenges of life—these have a most enfeebling effect on a minister's witness and character. They were never more out of place than to-day. A generation that has faced the daily, deadly menace of war will have little mercy on a merely cloistered ministry. To a young sculptor who came to Michael Angelo, anxious that the statue he had just completed should be seen in the best light, the Master replied: "Do not trouble too much about the light on your statue; the light of the public square will test its value." I have dwelt at some length on this peril of self-preoccupation, because I believe it is a very real pitfall for some of the most earnest spirits in our calling. Neither in the ministry nor in life are we at peace till we get ourselves off our own hands. We are not to be intent on cultivating, still less on exhibiting, our character like a prize dahlia. Of that rare suffering spirit, Giles Winterbourne, Hardy makes his lover say: "He was a good man and did good things." Our Lord Himself "went about doing good". He believed in no type of spirituality which was not instantly harnessed to deeds of service. How perfectly blended were His prayer life and His active life we can sense from saying after saying in the New Testament. "In the daytime He was teaching in the temple. At eventide He abode in the mount." This perfect rhythm may be beyond our human achieving, but we can "follow after".

There is another consideration which vitally affects our preaching. It is *the wise acceptance of our outward conditions* in the ministry. There is no more common illusion in our profession than the conviction that we could be a shining success anywhere else than in the sphere which we happen to be occupying. Granted that, in reasonable time or in special circumstances, a change may be good for a man and even better for his congregation, the fact remains that it is fatally easy to tire too early amid the ordinary difficulties of our task, and to pass our days in a state of sour querulousness which is anything but conducive to contagious preaching. The charge that is without its discouragements has yet to be discovered. Get it wrought into the fibres of your being that the sphere in which you find yourself is the arena in which you are to win your soul. Here, as elsewhere in life, the remedy is largely in our own hands. Emerson says of Socrates that "when he entered the prison, he took away all ignominy from the place, which could not be a prison while he was there". No surer Nemesis overtakes a man than that which visits a minister who considers himself thrown away on the people whom he has been called to serve, in the belief that they cannot appreciate the best preaching he has to give. It is in this connection that Dr. Maltby once said: "Don't talk down to your congregation. They are not there." It is an obvious corollary that, having accepted our outward conditions, we must also learn to except ourselves, men perfect only in our imperfection, strangely mingled of strength and weakness, of good and evil. This means that we are definitely and finally to accept our own temperament. Even after all that the grace of Jesus Christ had done for Peter and John, Peter was still Peter, and John was still John. Our natures may seem to be forever fluctuating between two extremes, easily elated and as easily depressed. It is not too much to say that this is precisely "the preacher's temperament". Exultation and humiliation may be the price we have to pay for the travail that goes with constant, emotional expenditure. Whatever be our temperament, we can always be ourselves, sincere and natural. We were not meant to go through this ever-changing world with a fixed smile on our faces. As has been well said: "The person who is incapable of depression depresses us, as the friend who is incapable of boredom bores us." It is necessary to come to terms with ourselves and God on these matters. Let us accept the faculties God has given us, nor lament too much those denied us. "God gives you the tools. You finish the job."

Again, character and preaching are so vitally related that we must see to it that, cost what it may, we shall preserve the citadel of our own hearts. Our service to others is, of course, the supreme concern of our ministry. That means that, in the best sense, we must be all things to all men. We must pray for a wide tolerance as we face the endless variety of character and temperament in those we serve. A man may have outstanding gifts of scholarship or character and yet be woefully lacking in the art of making human contacts. It is perilous, in this connection, for any minister to pride himself on the fact that he has no "small talk". Frankly, this can be sheer snobbery. If we are really anxious to get alongside our people, we must continually exert ourselves to be interested in the details of family life which make up the greater part of everyone's existence. The fact remains that a minister must strive to retain, amid all his geniality and friendliness, a certain solitude of spirit. There is a deep and subtle saying in the Book of Deuteronomy: "Take heed that thou offer not thy burnt offerings in every place thou seest." Of one of her characters, George Eliot says: "Her heart was a common highway." Of one of his, Mark Rutherford says: "There was no holy of holies within him to which one or two of the elect could be admitted and find God to be there." It is for this inviolable sanctuary that I am pleading. There is such a thing as having no resources for solitude. The possession of these is one of the prime necessities of the true preacher. One who saw John Henry Newman walking slowly round the quadrangle of Oriel College murmured: "Nunquam minus solus, quam cum solus" —"Never less alone than when alone." Let us beware both of the overbusyness and the garrulousness that make us incapable of bearing our own company. This is the citadel of our being where God reveals to us an original and authentic vision of Himself which will

88

shine forth in our preaching. In the words of Ecclesias-
ticus: "Make the counsel of thine own heart to stand,
for a man's mind is sometimes wont to bring him
tidings more than seven watchmen that sit on a high
tower." Out of this brooding, fruitful solitariness shall
we be able to say to our hearers: "I delivered unto you
that which I also received."

One unfaltering process will more and more pervade
the motions and activities of our inmost life as we
strive to be preachers owned and used of God. It is
the ceaseless quest for *truth of character and of speech*.
There is a sardonic sentence of Augustine Birrell which
is most relevant in this connection. "We have all
known many a sorry scrub who has fairly argued himself
into the belief that it is only his intellectual difficulties
that have prevented him from being another St.
Francis. We think we could suggest a few score other
obstacles." One defect at least we must strive at all
costs to eradicate from our inmost life, and that is our
refusal to call certain tendencies by their proper names.
If we did so, we would find that many of our enfeebling
depressions and so-called intellectual doubts are nothing but hidden disobediences to the heavenly vision,
cowardly refusals to follow our divinest insights and
intuitions; concealed compromises and treacheries that
sap the very foundations of character. God makes
Himself manifest to the man who follows, with utter
abandon, the light he already possesses. In a broadcast
on Dr. Johnson, the late Professor George Gordon

drives home this primary lesson. "To think Johnson," he says, "is, very simply, to have a habit of truth. It is, in all situations, to insist on the facts and to face them when found. It is to refuse, at whatever cost, to make life seem better than it is. It is to clear the mind of cant. No man can have lived long who thinks this habit common. No one has tried it who thinks it easy." Let us seek, as preachers, to acquire this inner realism and in our choice of words, in the stark honesty of our thoughts, and in the deepening purification of our own souls, our hearers will reap a constant spiritual harvest.

I go on to make a plea for what one might call "*the quiet mind*" about our preaching—and that in various directions. If it is, in the deepest sense, our very own, it will rid us once and for all of the demon of jealousy. Surely we have reached rock-bottom in our spiritual life when it gives us a pang to feel that another can make the Gospel of the Son of God a more wonderful blessing than we can. The only cure for this malady is to dwell more humbly and fervidly on the same Gospel and find grace to say:

> I love a thing that's fine
> Although it be not mine.
> Yea, though it never mine may be,
> Still it delights and comforts me.

And as it is wise to have a serene mind regarding the scope of our preaching, it were also wise to have a similar quietude regarding its effects. We are apt to envy the surgeon who continually sees the results of his labours. And indeed it must be a thrilling experience to see a man walking the streets in buoyant health who owes it, under God, to a gifted surgeon's skill. But it is the very romance of our calling that we walk by faith and not by sight. Let us put away for ever the temptation to self-tormenting anxiety about the consequences of our preaching. Let us have no post-mortems, especially in the physical depletion of a Sunday night. Once uttered, our message is taken up by the hand of God, to vaster issues than we can ever know. "He walks far who sees a word home."

> See how the ringing ripples spread
> Wider and wider evermore.
> God knows what word at random said
> Shall reach at last the eternal shore.

You will have comforting glimpses of the working of these spiritual laws when, years after you have preached a sermon, some perfect stranger may divulge to you that, in his case, the word was not yours but an intimate, thrilling, authentic word of God in some hour of desperate need. The laws of successful preaching are truly mysterious. We must learn to face with composure the fact that the sermon on which we have toiled and sweated almost unto blood, may seem in our eyes an abject failure, while a sermon of whose penury we are secretly ashamed may, by the merciful intervention of God, become, in His Hands, mighty to save. He would be a foolish man who would draw any hasty conclusion from this mystery. The practical inference is to sit down ever more doggedly to our task, convinced that, in the last resort the success of our ministry does not depend on a few brilliant efforts but on the general level of our preaching and on "the intention of our soul".

My final word would be this: *"Come what may, cling to your call."* Return again and again, like Abraham of old, to "the altar which you made at the first". A man's call to the ministry is something sacred and incommunicable. There is profound mystery in the steps by which the one life we have to live becomes pledged to our high calling. Our Christian homes, our parents, less by what they did and said than by what they were, shepherded us, albeit unconsciously, towards that ineffable moment when the call became irresistible. Add to this the influence, at an impressionable period, of a beloved minister or an inspired teacher, the timely reading of a great biography, the deepening effect of an illness, some strange intervention in the plans we had made for entering another career—all these working cumulatively experiences too tenuous to estimate, brought us, it may be, to the place where we surrendered ourselves for ever to the compulsion of the still, small voice. These are life's supreme memories, to which it were treachery to be finally unfaithful. It was of such experiences that Masefield wrote: "Life's an affair of instants spun to years." I shall never forget examining, some years ago, a young student for licence. Having asked him the prescribed questions, I passed him on to my colleague, a godly old elder. "Mr. —," he said quietly, "I have but one question to ask. Are you sure of your call?" With deep intensity, the youth replied: "If there is one thing in heaven and earth of which I am sure, it is that." As a man far on in the ministry, the words filled me with something between envy and questioning wonder, for I would be untrue to my responsibility in these lectures did I not warn you of the inevitable reactions to this first, fine rapture. There are black days ahead, when you will find yourself asking: "After all, have we been stampeded by a youthful emotion or parental pressure into a career for which we now fear we are hopelessly unfitted?" The first sacramental exhilaration subsides. The human nature we are to study and influence can be desperately intractable. There is no end to the travail of trying to fathom it. Then—the grimmest problem of all—our own poor advertisement for the Gospel we preach. The battle goes sore against us "to the going down of the sun". How, through the long, trying years, are we to maintain the spiritual glow? What is to happen when our ministry loses the fervour of gloriously working out what God has mysteriously worked in? How can the defeatist mood be turned to victory?

With the imprimatur of hundreds of ministers on what I say, my answer would be: *learn to believe what the years teach you against the days*. The verdict of the single day is often misleading and inaccurate. One day raises us to the heights; the very next may depress us to the depths. Not so the years. Let every minister who has held bravely to it, 'gainst storm and wind and tide, lift up his voice and answer: "If there is one thing of which we are confident it is this—that, down the years, the miracle of miracles is being wrought in us by the grace of God, this grace wherein we stand." It is we who can tell how, "when our lives hung by a hair of the mercy of God", that mercy stood the strain. For our countless needs, in the order of their coming, God has continued to send the timely reinforcements and the issue out of our afflictions. The fears of spiritual famine, natural to the young preacher, have been foreseen by One Who has led us by the green pastures and still waters of an ever-deepening experience. So has it been with the "plague of our own hearts", that hidden warfare from which there is to be no demobilisation. As Dr. Gossip puts it: "God has met our sin with grace, our added sin with added grace, our obstinate sin with obstinate grace, determinedly, stubbornly, persistently." Believing, then, what the years teach us against the days, we older men bid you be of good heart as you face the prospect of preaching the Gospel of hope in a dark, uncertain world. Speaking for myself, when my light burns low, I like to regale myself with certain sayings that, at breaking-point, rally me like a trumpet call. One of the greatest sayings in our greatest biography came not from Dr. Johnson himself, but from a plain old man, a former schoolmate, whom he met by chance in a London street. "I have tried, too, in my time to be a philosopher, but I don't know how, cheerfulness was always breaking in." Like thousands of others who have accepted the call to the Christian ministry, perhaps unlike many others in being constitutionally unable, in a world like this, to accept a facile optimism, one can but testify, looking back on the long years, that "cheerfulness has always been breaking in". Is not this the supreme attraction of the character of the great apostle? Dark as were his horizons, he had the gift of the morning star. It shines forth from every page he wrote. "We are troubled on every side, yet not distressed. We are perplexed, but not in despair; persecuted, but not forsaken; cast down, but not destroyed." Here was a man subjected to never-ending pains and necessities who yet saw his inner life as a series of divine resurrections. The stimulus towards this well-grounded hopefulness is a perennial one—your own warm, personal love to Jesus Christ, the Son of God. You go forth to all that awaits you, not because you have signed a formal creed. You can no more imprison the living, loving Christ in a creed than you can capture a perfume in a net. Deeper far than all that is speculative and merely intellectual is your personal calling in Christ Jesus—the fact that you are "Christ's man". And what follows from that? It is said that, when Garibaldi led his infantry against the Austrians, he never looked round to see if his men were following. He knew, to a dead certainty, that at the moment when he reached the enemy he would feel his men's breath hot on the back of his neck. It is with a like conviction that you are honoured and trusted by the Captain of your salvation. Our coming together in this place will not have been wholly vain if it has done something to rekindle the flame of your devotion to Christ in its pristine purity and ardour. May it burn through the years with ever-growing intensity, to the glory of God and the blessing of your fellow-men, and may yours be in the end an abundant entrance into the heavenly kingdom.